All Scripture references taken from the KJV of the Holy Bible unless otherwise indicated.

Demonic Time Bombs

by Dr. Marlene Miles

https:// marlenemilestheauthor.com

Freshwater Press 2023

ISBN: 978-1-960150-78-3

Paperback Version

Copyright 2023 by Dr. Marlene Miles

All rights reserved. No part of this book may be reproduced, distributed or transmitted by any means or in any means including photocopying, recording or other electronic or mechanical methods without prior written permission of the publisher except in the case of brief publications or critical reviews.

Contents

- Demonic Time Bombs 3
- Slow Weapons 5
- Weapons of the Flesh 19
- Accursed Things 26
- Life Is a Warfare 29
- Nothing In Me 32
- Grandma & Grandpa 34
- The Arameans 39
- Seasons Change 55
- Reactivation 57
- Monitoring Spirits 63
- The Accursed Thing 66
- I Have Prayed for You 68
- Pray, It's Your Birthday 72
- Destiny Clock 77
- Suddenly 80
- Prayers 84
- Christian books by this author: 96

Demonic Time Bombs

> No weapon that is formed against thee shall prosper and every tongue that shall rise against thee in judgment thou shalt condemn this is the heritage of the servants of the Lord and their righteousness is of me sayeth the Lord. (Isaiah 54:17)

We love to say that no weapon formed against us shall prosper. It is the Word of God; therefore, it is true.

The devil's got **weapons** that he's been using over and over on humans because humans are *humans*. We must learn, study the tactics of the devil, teach them to our children, and to others so we don't fall for the same evil tricks, repeatedly. If we would wise up we wouldn't fall into his traps.

Time bombs have a time of activation. They have been designed to go off at a particular time to kill, maim, devastate, or annihilate. Terrorists use them. Assassins use them. They are used in war. They are hidden with usually no one visible as it is set off. Don't be the one exclaiming, *I wasn't even doing anything – this just happened.* Nothing *just* happens. When it comes to time bombs, most victims do not suspect a thing—most don't see it coming.

If you are perfect and sin free, or you think you are, then you are deceived. By no fault of your own, a time bomb can be the result of ancestral and generational sin. Still, know that none of us are perfect.

We need to be sure that we are not part of the effort in the devil's forming of a weapon against us. If one has already been created generationally, we have to work to defuse it so it doesn't devastate our lives, or the lives of our children.

Slow Weapons

The devil has all kinds of weapons. He's got sudden weapons of destruction. But he also has slow weapons, some taking generations to form. The very same weapons have been used on your ancestors for decades, because what the devil is dishing out, the people in your bloodline, or mankind in general, are susceptible to. The same weapons that have been used over and again for centuries, may be waiting in the wings for you. You've got to do something about it.

We learned in Genesis that the serpent is subtle; we know that he uses hidden weapons that have been sneakily formed. There may be generational weapons such as the *like father like son* kind. Genetic issues are embedded in families as demonic time bombs.

I know of a man who lost his life the exact same way his father lost his life at the exact same rather young age. The entire family knew of this "generational medical issue," but the son was resistant to doing anything medically about it, even though he was aware of it, but in denial that it could be also happening to him.

No weapon formed against us should be **able** to prosper, but we have to do our part by learning about the weapons and taking correct and timely action against them.

Who, in reality would see a weapon and do nothing about it? No, we instinctively do something. Avoid it? Disarm it? Run from it? Tell someone?

Do something! We don't pick it up, inspect it, celebrate it, or bring it home. Normally.

In the case of this man, neither he nor his family did anything spiritually about the possibility of this exact same thing happening to him. But this exact thing happened to him. The one weapon the devil devised took out a father at 43 years old and then his son when the son was that same age. What about the grandson? Will they pray now? Or will they just *wait, and see*? Faith without works is not only dead, but it can also lead to death.

Faith is powerful and just because you hear bad news that something in your bloodline could be inherited by you doesn't mean that you will. But it also doesn't mean that you freeze in fear or in denial, and do nothing--, letting it happen. You must fight it spiritually, in prayer.

The devil has slow weapons such as time bombs that are waiting to ambush a person or a family.

In dentistry I hear people over and again say their crown came off and they were only eating bread, or something soft. They proclaim, *I wasn't even eating anything hard.* Many times, that's true. Biting on something hard breaks the cement seal that is keeping the crown on, but it is not until a person eats something soft that the crown is collected in that soft food and becomes dislodged from the tooth. In this way, they didn't even know that they had a problem or when the problem happened. They don't know until the thing they trusted in is no longer in place. And watch that crown become dislodged on the day you have to give a presentation at work, or you have an important dinner meeting, or it's the weekend or a holiday and you can't find your dentist.

The devil could hit a person really hard in the spirit--and they don't even know that something hit them. Then in the natural something seemingly easy comes along and they become aware of a deficit where they least expected it.

Weapons are often formed in the spirit, at night, while a person is asleep. Many times, when a person is careless, prayerless, and partying, a weapon could be formed against them. And they don't even know what happened, or that anything happened. Like a hard break, yet you don't know that anything broke until something soft pulls it away. When people sin on Friday night and nothing appears to have happened to them when they wake up on Saturday morning, they surmise that nothing will happen. That is not true. There are time bombs out there waiting for the best time to detonate.

Weapons formed against people are sometimes formed *inside* a person. How many house renovation shows have you seen where the outside of the house looks fine, but the timbers or joists on the inside, behind the walls are crumbling with rot? Time bombs.

Any of us could look amazing on the outside any day of the week, but what is happening on the inside of us, spiritually, emotionally, mentally, physically, silently and we either don't have a clue or we are bent on hiding it from the world, or even in denial, ourselves? Those are time bombs as well.

Some weapons are on the outside of the intended victim, plainly obvious, right in our faces. Cousin Jr. lives next door; you see him several times a week. You also know that he is jealous of you and is scheming against you whenever he can. Or, you have a co-worker who keeps trying to get you in trouble by sabotaging your work. You've got your eye on them both. Those are close weapons trying to form against you.

Don't pick a fight with either of them; put your prayer life on them and let God be God and handle these characters for you.

Both the aforementioned weapons are close to us.

Weapons at a distance can come from you don't even know where or who. A person does not have to know you to hate you. They just hate. The devil has assigned them to hate, so that's what they do. They don't even know you. When we are young and stupid, we try to find out why people hate us and either change ourselves to make them like us, or we try to change their minds about us. When we are older and less stupid, we don't do that; we know that some people simply hate. Period. And there is nothing you can do or change about yourself to make them like you. Ever.

Slow weapons, sudden weapons, close weapons, distant weapons, inside weapons, outside weapons--, weapons from known folks and from strangers -, that's a serious menu of weapons that the devil has.

Fear not, we have a full-*er* menu of spiritual warfare weapons against him; ours are greater, mightier and more assured if we will but use the weapons that God has provided for us. God never loses a battle, and we are not designed to lose either, as long as we are ***in Christ***.

One serious weapon the devil uses to place on the inside of us and is potentially devastating to man is spirit food. We should be as concerned, or more concerned to get *spiritual* food--, evil spiritual food out of us as we are to keep natural food moving through and out of the body. Not only is spirit food defiling, but it is also dangerous, and can be deadly.

When you see yourself eating **anything** in a dream, that is the result of an evil caterer. In the dream, when you are handed things to eat and you are putting them in your mouth, that is dangerous. Seems harmless; it's not. I have prayed to God and He obliges me. **Lord, if I am asleep and I am given spiritual food, or I am about to eat spirit food, or have eaten or drank anything – <u>anything</u>--, Lord, wake me up immediately!**

I wake up and immediately I spit out, (symbolically) vomit up, reject spirit food, in the Name of Jesus. I state: *I remove your power and all residual effects on me by the power in the Blood of Jesus.* I declare that it will not have any effect on me now, or into the future. Return to sender. Provider of this evil food, eat your own food and die, in the Name of Jesus.

Really, have you ever thought that God created us to live and have life more abundantly, but the devil is about trying to kill man, by any means. People who are suddenly sick, devastatingly ill, chronically ill--, have any of us really thought about the spiritual aspects of illness and why mankind is so sick? It's devil-work, of course.

Spirit food hides in the human body, and it is a weapon that is formed against humans that can be detonated by the devil. It is **not** really food. It is nothing that should be consumed; it is an evil initiation, and it is a time bomb. Furthermore, we are spirits, spirits don't need to EAT. So, do you even know what this "food" is that is being handed to you? What does it taste like? What's the texture? Don't know. I don't think anyone knows; I've never met anyone who can describe it. We just know that it is demonic, and it can be programmed and even timed to blow up on you. Feels like things moving around in your body? That's one of the results of having consumed spirit food that is still in there.

The recipient of spirit food must be prayerful and wise to get rid of it, nullify its effects, vomit and/or expel it, also spiritually before the devil ambushes that person using any number of ways because of what has been deposited into the victim.

No Weapon formed? Okay, you've got to know what the weapons are in order to know if they've been or are being established or fashioned against you. Evil *spirit* food is a **time bomb.**

Pray the Lord will put a hedge of protection around you especially in your dream life while you are asleep, and the enemy is trying to feed you evil spirit food. I pray that for you, in the Name of Jesus.

Be diligent to track, record and know what your dreams mean. Make sure you are not **eating**, in the dream, drinking in the dream. having sex in the dream. We spend as much as 1/3 of our lives asleep. While asleep we are in the spirit; we must learn what dreams really mean and handle our lives prayerfully. For example, seeing dead relatives or friends or things in the dream is very bad. These are all initiations into hell and hellish covenants. There are others, but I wanted to mention these.

We are very worried in the natural about regular **bowel** movements and to keep everything moving through the body, getting waste materials out of us. Cleanses, water flushes, saunas, fiber, even laxatives and other treatments are used, even abused to keep food in the natural that we've eaten flowing through and out of us. Granted, most people just want to lose or maintain weight. But we don't want to hold on to food, especially that has been converted to waste for too long. People go on fasts of all kinds. It is more critical that spirit food has to go!

Not eating is a fast. If you pray, read your Bible and honor God while you are fasting then that is a proper **Godly** fast. If you don't pray during a fast, do all your usual stuff, watch movies, listen to all kinds of music, et cetera, then it is not a fast dedicated to God. That is an evil fast. I could say you're just on a diet and that is partly true, but witches fast. So, there is such a thing as an evil fast.

Fasts are very useful spiritually and it renews our strength and health according to Isaiah 58:6. If your fast is not dedicated to God and properly observed, it defaults to a diet or an evil fast. Don't let what you're doing be your undoing. Don't let your good be evil spoken of (in the spirit).

Weapons of the Flesh

Every work of the flesh is either the beginning, the building or the completion of a weapon against the **sinner** who is operating in his or her flesh. Read carefully: When you are working in the flesh, you are creating a weapon against **yourself**, not against the person that you hate. You may be using your flesh self to enact a physical assault of some kind against the object of your disdain. It could be an emotional or soulish weapon against another human, but all the while you are creating a *spiritual* weapon against **yourself**. What you can *see* is not all there is.

For example, you've chosen not to forgive Uncle Boopsy, so you don't take his calls, or help him mow the lawn anymore like you used to. That'll show him, *won't it?* But your hatred is creating an invisible spiritual weapon that is aimed directly at **you**, not Uncle.

You are creating a flesh weapon in the natural and a worse spiritual weapon is simultaneously being created against you because of your own actions. Which weapon do you think is more powerful? The physical weapon or the spiritual weapon? Still, we say, *No weapon formed against us…*

Flesh weapons are most devastating because the sinner is invested into the weapon. By not forgiving, for example, *Sinner Man* is doubling down, both helping to create the weapon, and also saying that he is not willing to **dismantle** the weapon, or at least *help* in dismantling a weapon, even if he is standing before a deliverance minister at that very moment. The deliverance worker: apostle, prophet, pastor, et cetera, cannot cast anything out against a person's will. If the evil *spirit* would even go, most likely it won't--, that would be witchcraft. We force nothing against a person's will.

They say you will not confess a thing until you are finished with it. When someone is keeping something or someone a secret, they are not done with them yet. Once they begin to freely talk about it to those who need to know, then we all know that the "relationship" has run its course and the person is ready to, or has finally let go. That is the basis for salvation. That is the basis of repentance. That is the first step in substance recovery. That is the first step to deliverance.

If you hold on to unforgiveness and unforgiveness is tethering that demon or weapon to you, you will keep that demon.

> The acts of the flesh are obvious: sexual immorality, impurity and debauchery; idolatry and witchcraft; hatred, discord, jealousy, fits of rage, selfish ambition, dissensions, factions and envy; drunkenness, orgies, and the like. I warn you, as I did before, that those who live like this will not inherit the kingdom of God.(Galatians 5:19-21 NIV)

I hope you don't want to know which work of the flesh creates which weapon against the sinner so you can decide if it is worth it or that you'll risk going into the flesh because maybe the weapon created won't be so bad. Oh please. Whatever the work of the flesh is, the very same door that you opened is the one that will work against you. Whatever bad things can happen against you related to what work of the flesh you are working in, is more than likely what will happen. Notwithstanding, the proclivities and history of your bloodline will determine what things are available to go in the weapon that the devil will be creating for **you** while you are trying to create a weapon against *someone else*.

Let's say you have created a sling shot to fling evil words at Uncle Boopsy and malign his character and downgrade his reputation. The devil puts that sling shot on steroids and he now adds a spiritual power to do the same and much worse to you. *When* will he do it? Don't know. Even if not right away, it most likely still be a sudden attack-- when you least expect it, like a time bomb.

Because of this, most people don't even put it together that their hatred and campaign against Uncle

Boopsy was the cause of them being falsely accused at work and losing the best paying job they ever had, like a year later. In this way, it is hard to learn.

If you have a dog, for example, you can't punish your dog for chewing your new shoes last year, next year. There is no *connection* to the two events to your pet. The memory of man is far better than that of most animals, but man tends to forget. Unrepentant man especially has a tendency to forget because when a man is continuously sinning, he does not have a sorrowful heart. Instead, he becomes arrogant and self-righteous. He rationalizes that he was justified in treating Uncle Boopsy with disrespect and therefore if the sinner man can't see that he did anything wrong, what is there to remember? When the punishment comes for the crime, Sinner Man will be so confused, wondering, what happened here?

It is only with Godly sorrow, or at least guilt that a man may remember that he did Uncle Boopsy or anyone else for that matter, wrong, and he, being a sinner caused the destruction that is pursuing his life.

Accursed Things

You cannot stand against your enemies because of the accursed things. If you went into a store and put a store item into your pocket, you cannot stand against your accuser and prevail if that shoplifted item is on you. If there is a bank robbery or a worse crime and you have the weapon used in your possession, you will not prevail in court. It is the same as coming to court with dirty hands. If you are dirty, how can you accuse another of being dirty? In your obedience God punishes disobedience of others. Courts even require you present with clean hands.

If you had someone's car, don't you think they'd come to your house to get it? If you had someone's pet, and they knew you had it, wouldn't they come to get it? You may be looking at the things in your house and saying, *I bought this with my own money. This was given to me; it belongs to me.* You will about swear everything in your house **belongs** to you. It does in the natural. But in the spiritual world there are things that **belong** to the devil, to the marine kingdom, to New Age, to witchcraft, to pagan religions. Those things, although there are people who have the audacity or the ignorance to deal in them, sell them and buy them; they **belong** to certain spiritual entities.

Jesus said make no graven (engraved) image of God. Engraved images of idol *gods* "belong" to the idol *gods*. If you have those items in your possession, or in your house, it's rather an invitation for them to enter your domicile and your life. You get an idol of Diana or some random "saint," an evil eye, a pentagram ring –, even if you don't know what it is or where the image emanates from, it is still license for the entity (entities) associated with that item to come into your life. Further, they aren't leaving as long as that item is there and you may have to do much more work (deliverance) to get those evil *spirits* out of your life even after their paraphernalia is out of your house.

Consumed spirit food, or food in the natural dedicated to idols, food not prayed over are all defiling; they become as **accursed** things. This means your prayer life and your power in God is diminished if any of that is in you. God never intended for food, or beverage to be a curse to man.

Life Is a Warfare

Life is warfare, spiritually speaking, we don't war against flesh and blood, but life is a warfare. At work I notice people who believe they have nothing to do. There is plenty to do; they just don't know either how to do that job, how to work at all, or they are lazy and deceiving their employer for a paycheck for no or little work done.

Working out our salvation with fear and trembling is **work**. Faith without works is dead; that implies also *work*. Occupy until I return, means to **work**. The man who doesn't work should not eat. Study to show yourself approved is also **work**. Work is doing what you were sent to do, hired to do, or designed to do. Now if you *enjoy* the work by help of the Holy Spirit, then amen. But the things you especially do not enjoy doing--, those things are **work**. We want God to "pay" us, but for what? Are we doing the **work**?

Washing dishes for me is work; cooking is not. I still have to wash dishes, or at least make sure they are washed. I work.

Many Christians have said that they are a soldier in the Army of the Lord – *soldiering* is work. **Warfare is work.** Being an intercessory prayer warrior is work. There are times that you could be sleeping or relaxing, but you are praying.

My pastor says, *Unless you are doing what you were sent here to do, you are not prospering,* that is, you are not in prosperity. **Work leads to prosperity. Period.**

Warfare includes studying and if you don't like to read, especially your Bible, and you don't like to pray then that will be **work** for you. Each bit of spiritual work you do adds to the power of your own "bomb" that you can detonate against the enemy when he comes in like a flood against you. Bombs sometimes take time to build; they are not always instant. Pay attention, do your work. Whether or not you study the enemy and know his tactics, know this: he is surely studying you—has been since you were born.

Look at what's looking at you. The devil has been studying us. It's not because he loves us, no he hates us. Because the devil has declared war on mankind, there is work to do.

Nothing In Me

Monitoring spirits study us to see what we are doing. We can pray, *Forget my name, lose my location* to our heart's content. But we need to be self-aware: The ownness is on us – yeah, we want to pray against what's looking at us, that is, **we** need to walk upright before the Lord, that the enemy doesn't **find** anything in us that he can use as an open door, as an opportunity to attack, that is, steal, kill, or destroy.

Walk circumspectly: Walk in Wisdom

See then that you walk circumspectly, not as fools but as wise, redeeming the time, because the days are evil. Therefore do not be unwise, but understand what the will of the Lord *is,* (Ephesians 5:15-17).

We can't just go through life doing any thing we want to do and then get angry because God is not protecting us from the iniquity that follows sin. Sin & death is a law – if you sin, stuff is just coming at you. When we sin, we must repent quickly and thank God there is forgiveness and the Blood of Jesus. We do not use Grace as an opportunity to sin, thinking the Blood of Jesus will cover us from whatever we want to do.

We must walk circumspectly, so, on any given day when God looks at you, what will He see?

On any given day when the devil looks, sends *monitoring spirits* to report back—what will those reports be like?

Grandma & Grandpa

We are often curious to know which of our ancestors we look like. Whose nose is this, why am I this tall or this short. We compare complexion and hair type to our living and deceased relatives. We inherit physical traits from our parents, grandparents, great grandparents and beyond; and we seem to care so much about inherited physical traits.

When they see certain traits that they don't care for in their child, parents are quick to say, *You're just like your daddy*. Or, *You've got your momma's tempe*r. Any and all of that could be true, and they are not just talking points. Things that are *just like* momma, or *just* *like* daddy but are not **just like God** need to be dealt with. The things in any of us that are not **JUST LIKE GOD** are the things that are purchase points for the devil. They are the things that he can latch a hook into and try to gaffe any human.

So, we must walk circumspectly. We should respectfully look at our parents and ancestors, not to condemn them, but to evaluate and weigh out their behaviors as a way of mapping what *spirits* that are not the Holy Spirit, are in them and therefore in the household and culture we grew up in and therefore what might be in us.

For example, my dad never met a mirror that he didn't LOVE, therefore I am keen to pray against that for myself and not become that same way. It's not funny or cute because Dad was that way; it's not funny or cute if it is not *like*

God. It is especially nothing to be cherished if it is a work of the flesh, or demonic.

One parent may be keen to try to drive out the behaviors in their child from the other parent that they hate, because they can clearly see it. The other parent is objective to the spouse's shortcomings, but cannot see their own. Herein lies human foibles.

> And why beholdest thou the **mote** that is in thy brother's eye, but considerest not the beam that is in thine own eye?
>
> Or how wilt thou say to thy brother, Let me pull out the **mote** out of thine eye; and, behold, a beam is in thine own eye?
>
> Thou hypocrite, first cast out the beam out of thine own eye; and then shalt thou see clearly to cast out the **mote** out of thy brother's eye. (Matthew 7:3-5)

This is why, especially as two become *one* they encourage one another, admonish one another and tell each other the truth <u>in Love</u>. Therefore, there is no condemnation in this **love** relationship. If you can't love the one who loves you, what have you? If the person you love can't tell you that you have spinach stuck between your teeth and you don't go off, then that speaks to the need for deliverance. Truth in love is one of the ways relationships grow, last, and flourish.

Parents, your beautiful child— look at your mom and dad, look at your spouse's mom and dad and grands, there are so many traits to choose from. You will not magically get only the best traits *(spirits)* from your respective bloodlines. You know—the ones you like. We have to look past the flesh, yeah, your child is cute--, it is rare that a child is not cute in appearance and behavior. But teething starts, they may become grumpy. Terrible two's are terrible. Three-year-olds who follow you everywhere, even to the bathroom and by the time a child is 5 years old they re ready to take over the house. Not having a five-year-old run your house is exactly why five-year-olds don't have their own houses, or children.

The Arameans

Second Kings 6:8-23 tells the story of how Elisha trapped blinded Arameans.

Now the king of Aram was at war with Israel. After conferring with his officers, he said, "I will set up my camp in such and such a place."

The man of God sent word to the king of Israel: "Beware of passing that place, because the Arameans are going down there."

So the king of Israel checked on the place indicated by the man of God. Time and again Elisha warned the king, so that he was on his guard in such places.

This enraged the king of Aram. He summoned his officers and demanded of them, "Tell me! Which of us is on the side of the king of Israel?"

> "None of us, my lord the king," said one of his officers, "but Elisha, the prophet who is in Israel, tells the king of Israel the very words you speak in your bedroom."

God is Omnipresent; He is everywhere all at once. He knows everything that is going on. Period. God may choose to reveal something to His prophets, or a person. Any person can ask God something and God may answer. You don't have to be a prophet, or stand in the office of a prophet or anything like that. You can just *ask God* something about the tactics of the enemy that is up against you and God can tell you. He can even tell you what the enemy has planned behind your back or in any secret place.

If there is a purpose to you knowing a thing and you're going to do something appropriate and Godly about it, I'm sure God will tell you if you ask and sit still long enough to hear from Him.

Verse 13: "Go, find out where he is," the king ordered, "so I can send men and **capture** him." The report came back: "He is in Dothan."

The devil is **not** omnipresent. He has to send imps and spies and *monitoring spirits* to find out things about you. Then those *spirits* go back to file reports to their master, the devil.

Once the devil knows your whereabouts and as much else as he can find out, he either continues to strategize against you, continue working on the device he has against you, or makes a plan to detonate.

Back to the King of Aram--,

Verse 14: Then he sent horses and chariots and a strong force there. They went by night and surrounded the city.

Elisha was still praying and prayerful so when he woke up the next morning and looked outside. Because God was still talking to Elisha and Elisha was still talking to God, Elisha was not surprised or taken off guard by the army that came for him.

You, as a prayerful Christian may have also asked God about the plans of the enemy against you, and when you got up the next morning and looked outside, you would not have been surprised either. Looking in Verse 15, Elisha's servant was surprised, but Elisha was not taken aback.

Verse 15: When the servant of the man of God got up and went out early the next morning, an army with horses and chariots had surrounded the city. "Oh no, my lord! What shall we do?" the servant asked.

One morning in a quiet suburban cul-de-sac, in Bible Belt, America, of all places, still in my pj's, I got up and looked outside. It was about 5am, barely daybreak, and my *then*-husband was loud and in a phone fight with his ex-wife. These fights were commonplace, and it had gotten old--, day one. Two years into his second marriage--, the one with me, they were still at it. What was it *this time?* The mother of the 7-year-old with whom he shared custody was outside the house to pick the child up from a weekend with his father, on their way to a family holiday.

Outside? Glad you asked that. There were three or four car- and SUV-loads of people in summer road trip gear because they were all going to Disney World to see Mickey. As I learned, the convoy was set to meet and then leave at 5am from outside the boy's father's house. First I'd heard of this, but I most often had no knowledge of what the *then*-husband was planning regarding ***his*** child.

However, his ex's arrival with her entire family wasn't a surprise to the husband because, as I came to learn later, the ex-wife had asked him at least two weeks earlier, but he was insistent on resisting her request. *As per usual.*

The only problem was-- **everything**. The dad, my *then*-husband said that his "visitation" with the child was not over until 7am and the son was still asleep--, he wasn't. Cars and SUV's full of people? Yes, that was a lot of people, but the boy's mother's family was not the only ones who had surrounded the house. Unbeknownst to me there had been several calls made to the police by those outside and maybe even neighbors, for all I knew. Two police cruisers had arrived.

In addition to that, there had been calls made to the house from the policemen there, and the boy's father had answered the police and told them, whatever he had told them—probably that he had two more hours left on his visitation and the boy was asleep. The child was vertical, walking about the house and probably wanted to go with the vacationers, but he was not a dumb kid; he had learned early, often being coached and given everything he wanted by his *dad*, how to manage his dad and not let on that he really wanted out of that house.

There were 4 officers outside having arrived in the two marked police cars. The reluctance of the dad to send the child out was seen as a hostage situation by the police.

A document came over the house FAX machine. In large black type like a kidnapper's ransom note, it read: **You have 5 minutes to release the boy to the mother or a SWAT team will descend upon the residence.** I wondered if I should call my mother to say goodbye, because I knew whom I had married by this time, and geez--, a SWAT team. How do you get out of this?

It was obvious that the mother hadn't sent the fax, she was standing outside by her car on the street, with the rest of her family, so her relatives hadn't sent it either. Furthermore, the technology to send a FAX from other than a FAX did not exist at that time.

Yeah, this really happened.

If this wasn't a time bomb, then you tell me what is. The FAX seemed like a viable heads up from the police, or someone who knew what the police were planning. I asked the then-husband, *Why don't you let him go on out so he can go on vacation with his mom and uncles and aunts and cousins?*

He dismissed me. He was determined to wait until 7am.

Verse 16: "Don't be afraid," the prophet answered. "Those who are with us are more than those who are with them."

I must stop here to let you know that there were **more** outside than were with us inside that house and especially with a SWAT team expected. God wasn't in this mayhem, so He surely was not responsible to send Heavenly support to keep a child from going on vacation with his family. This *dad* didn't have a leg to stand on because he was being unreasonable and stubborn for no real reason.

You cannot stand against your enemy when you are harboring something that you should not be harboring. Can a *person* be an accursed thing? The firstborn male that opens the womb is to be dedicated to God. This child was a firstborn male who had opened the womb of his birth mother. Some things should not be or remain in your house, especially when they should not be there, **timewise.**

Dude-husband, whom I trusted to be my spiritual covering had ***helped*** the devil create a flesh-weapon that could easily backfire on him because of his unforgiveness, bitterness, animosity against the ex. Simply because I was also in that house, I could have also been in harm's way.

The people outside were **not enemies**, at least not mine. But at any time, and especially in today's climate, having police think that you are holding a person against their will, or against the word of the Court is criminal and extremely dangerous. From my understanding, the two "ex's" had been fighting each other over the child and how to raise him since they had adopted him as a newborn, and that was also a time bomb in the making. Was this the day it would explode? Only God knew.

Saints of God, order your steps. Ask the Lord to order your steps so you are not collateral damage in <u>someone else's</u> time bomb if it is detonated. Sometimes in our unsanctioned *mercy* we run to the side of someone who has established a **time bomb** or multiple time bombs because we think we can *save* them.

Jesus saves.

We pray, and using Wisdom, we stay out of harm's way. We need to let Jesus be Jesus. Let Jesus do the saving.

Eventually two policemen were allowed in the house. They asked me to step outside. I refused. I told them, *I have nothing to do with this drama and I will not be humiliated by stepping outside in pj's in front of all those people.* They would not let me leave the room we were in to get dressed. But they also could not force me to go outside, either. Truthfully, if I had stepped outside, they could have arrested me out there. In my house they could do nothing to me.

After I told them that this did not involve me, the Lord "blinded" the eyes of the cops in the house so they stopped looking at me and paid attention to the overzealous *dad* who wouldn't release a 7-year-old to go to Disney Land on a hot day in August during the child's summer vacation.

It's many years later and I have just realized that if I had stepped outside what might they have done with that man that I had married who was trying to hide his belligerence with a soft voice and calm, calculated words? Had he himself **become** his own time bomb? When a man becomes his own time bomb, that is some serious devil success.

Around 6am the child was *released* to go see Mickey, and the convoy quietly pulled out. The other two cops came in the house and all four stayed for another ½ hour or so to make sure this man was calm. Now, I suppose they stayed to make sure I was okay. They even asked me that. I assured them I was not afraid. In their staying, God made sure that there were more with me than were with the devil in the *then*-husband.

That husband? We divorced. Not that day, but *yeah*...

How many times did Jesus escape a mob that wanted to stone, or throw Him from a high hill?

In that cul-de-sac that hot summer morning, the devil wanted humiliation, the family mob outside would have been the audience. A SWAT team? Lord Jesus, help. And that's a real prayer.

If the person or people **you** are with are endangering your physical or spiritual **life**, you need to reconsider where you are, who you're with, and also your own actions. There are people who can knowingly or unknowingly help the devil work evil against you, (or themselves) and even set up time bombs that they contribute to, but when it is detonated, they look completely innocent. You know the types who describe sudden disasters as, *I don't know what happened.* Or, *It just happened.*

Wherever the enemy has set up ambushes against you, with or without the help of witless or evil humans--, relatives, friends, exes, or strangers, May the Lord always be on your side.

May the Lord, blind them so they cannot see you and take them out of your presence and send them away, in the Name of Jesus.

If a time bomb has been set to detonate against you, may the Lord God of Elisha give you advance notice and protect you from all harm, in Jesus' Name.

May the God of Elisha send His prophet, send the Holy Spirit, or Lord, send Your Word so I will know ahead of time where the enemy has set up time bombs against you and you stay clear of those areas, in the Name of Jesus.

Seasons Change

The devil sets snares and traps that he has established against souls to set them off at some specific times of their lives. Sometimes he baits the trap to make it more enticing. He puts on the things you like. And the things you *like* will match the *spirit(s)* that are *in* you, they will have an affinity for each other. There will be a demonic **charge** and attraction, for the two to connect like attracting magnets. If you're greedy, look out for get-rich-quick schemes, they will come to you like water.

If you have a roving eye, if you're a lustful sort, the devil will send honey pot after honey pot, and he will make sure you see them. No, all women are not *like that–*, the **show,** that parade of scantily-clad females in front of your eyes is provided especially for you by your local *familiar spirit based on what you like and/or look at and for.* It is either to entice, entrap, or ensnare you. If it's what you've been praying for, you weren't praying to God. The devil answered because you were praying to him. You ask for something ungodly, God doesn't answer that, the prince of this world does.

This flesh show is not a gift, it's a trick, especially if you go to the places where these types of shows are held. Every misstep is part of the formation of, or the building up of a time bomb that the devil will use at the most opportune time for him and the most inopportune time for you.

Reactivation

The Lord is a warrior, the Lord is His name.

The devil is a copycat and a counterfeiter. If God is a warrior, what do you think the devil will try to be? The same thing. But the devil's version of being a warrior is to fight against man, while God is fighting **for** man.

The devil loves trauma, which in humans opens doors for the devil to get in. The devil is an assassin and he's involved in warfare against mankind with no regard to human life.

One of his choice weapons is the **time bomb** which he uses to devastate lives and destinies. They are bombs designed to explode at a particular **time** of a man's life, and beyond, as in generational time bombs. They could explode on a certain day, a certain week or month or a year – every year, for all we know, over and over every year, or month, week, or day maybe chosen to activate a tragedy bomb for someone or *reactivate* a tragedy. Time bombs can be detonated once or cyclically–, over and over again triggered by certain events in a family, or certain special days or dates. Curses and disasters programmed into the elements, such as the Triangular Powers will be of a repeating nature.

Fool me once? Lord, let it not be so, in the Name of Jesus. Amen.

The Sons of Isachaar could discern the times; Lord, let us have that Grace. Else, we may not know what days or dates to look out for, unless the Holy Spirit reveals it to us.

Any event can also be targeted to trigger an evil explosion in a person's life. Repent, and let God, and every evil time bomb along your path in life be supernaturally defused, in Jesus' Name.

Lord, let every explosive and critical situation planted and timed against my destiny, fail, in Jesus' Name.

Arrows of affliction, time bombs of affliction, every evil bomb of affliction set against me, fail to explode against me; return to sender, in the Name of Jesus.

Arrows of death, time bombs of death, every evil time bomb set against me; return to sender, in Jesus' Name.

Dirty garments of destruction--, all bombs of sudden destruction, all time bombs, fail against me, in Jesus' Name.

Time bombs of marital discord, fail against me; return to sender, in the Name of Jesus.

Time bombs of theft, failure, lack, insufficiency, and/or poverty, fail; be defused against me; return to sender, in the Name of Jesus.

Time bombs against my children, fail to explode, in the Name of Jesus.

Explosives planted and timed against my destiny, refuse to detonate, in the Name of Jesus.

Time bombs programmed into any Triangular Power or any Earthly or celestial element; be dismantled, be deprogrammed against me and return to sender, in the Name of Jesus. Explode in their face.

Art and tactics of war, work in my favor, in the Name of Jesus.

A sinner's attempt to bypass being able to discern the times is to reach out to a psychic. From our study passage, Elisha told the king over and again what the king of Aram was plotting, so much so that the king became paranoid and thought his men were working against him. *King,* they had said, *That prophet knows what you are saying in your own bedroom.*

Knowing what your enemy is doing or the best day or time to go abaout certain business is a gift from God. The ungodly sinner's work-around is to ask a witch, a diviner, or any of the 2nd heaven agents that God **hates**.

Nancy Regan advised her husband, the President of the United States by astrology and psychics on things such as the best day to do this, that or the other. This is the type of info diviners provide. Who do you think the astrologers that First Lady Nancy was talking to, *were talking to?* **Second heaven demons.**

Diviners are ever trying to bypass or outsmart God. They may not even believe that God is, or that He has any power. The Regan's son is an atheist who probably thinks it's his idea, but when visiting diviners, or using idol *gods*, there is always a hidden cost.

An evil enemy will go to a diviner multiple times, asking and paying every day, to learn, *what is the best day, time, hour to attack their victim.* Those who want to attack someone don't accidentally attack them; it will be well planned out, but in secret.

Lord, let there be no best day, no best time to attack me, in Jesus' Name.

Lord, give Your angels charge over me to keep me in all my ways, that there are no unguarded hours, in Jesus' Name.

Monitoring Spirits

Then one of the twelve, called Judas Iscariot, went unto the chief priests,

And said unto them, What will ye give me, and I will deliver him unto you? And they covenanted with him for thirty pieces of silver.

And from that time he sought opportunity to betray him. (Matthew 26:14-16)

Judas Iscariot became as a *monitoring spirit* against Jesus, seeking opportunity to betray Jesus Christ.

Lord, blind all *monitoring spirits* against me that they find nothing to report to their master, in Jesus' Name.

A girl with *a spirit of divination* followed the Disciples day after day, until Paul commanded the *spirit* to leave. The *spirit* instantly left the girl.

I bind all *spirits of divination* against me, my spouse, house, family, children and business, in the Name of Jesus. Go blind and deaf; forget my name, lose my location, in the Name of Jesus.

Lord, anyone following me, tracking what I'm doing or planning, whether they realize it or not, have them stop, lose my location, and forget my Name and their assignment against me, in the Name of Jesus.

Why would the devil be strategizing against you? Because *you've got it going on.* You've got an important role and purpose in the plan of God for mankind. God gave Joseph a dream, but Joseph told it to his brothers, who were evil, but Joseph didn't know that his brothers would go to the lengths they went to. The enemy used Joseph's brothers to try to kill him and his dream.

KEEP YOUR MOUTH SHUT. Protect yourself against *monitoring spirits*. Keep secret revelations and words from God to yourself. Stop telling all your business to everyone. What is between you and God is between you and God. Social media people, you make it so easy for your natural and spiritual enemies by posting all your business online. STOP IT!

The Accursed Thing

Lord, remove anything in me, any markers, any iniquity, any witchcraft in me that allows a curse of any kind to alight on me, or my bloodline, in the Name of Jesus.

Then it shall be *that* he who is taken with the accursed thing shall be burned with fire, he and all that he has, because he has transgressed the covenant of the LORD, and because he has done a disgraceful thing in Israel.'" (Joshua 7:15 NKJV)

Because of the accursed thing you cannot stand against your enemy.

Get all things accursed out of your camp, your house, your body, and life.

Plead the blood. Bind and rebuke them, renounce and denounce the sin that allows them to be in your life. Send them back to the pit, blind them, deafen them, in Jesus' Name.

I decree and declare to any enemy trying to establish a time bomb against me or my bloodline, I am not your candidate; I bear in my body the marks of the Lord Jesus; I am in Christ and He is in me.

I am not a candidate for affliction, death, theft, or destruction for the enemy.

I Have Prayed for You

The enemy of your soul is a strategist who is always looking for auspicious times and unguarded hours to strike. Mordecai and all the Jews both fasted and prayed to defuse the bomb that Haman had established against them, else, it would have exploded and all of them would have been wiped off the face of the Earth. God answered the prayer of the Jews and defused Haman's "bomb."

Jesus told Peter, **"Satan desires to sift you like wheat, BUT I HAVE PRAYED FOR YOU."**

The devil sifting like wheat? To me, that sounds like an evil cartoon character setting time bombs to blow people to smitherings.

Jesus, our Great Intercessor, makes intercession for us to the Father;– but we have to also pray.

I pray for you: God shall ambush every ambush against your life and destiny, in the Name of Jesus.

I pray and you also pray that the Lord will move you faster than your enemies.

Who are you hanging out with? The right people? People who pray for you? – With you? Then, you're more likely to fulfill destiny. Hanging out with the wrong crowd, the prayerless, the careless, the rebellious? Then you are more than likely <u>not</u> going to reach destiny. Bombs may be set for any day. Watch and pray, in the Name of Jesus. **Watch and pray** is part of the warfare. Have you ever noticed while dressing your character on a warfare or football video game that they just stand there and breathe? That's any man who puts on the whole armor of God and does nothing else after that. He's just standing there, breathing. Yes, put on the whole armor, then watch, pray, and do!!!

Remember, in your family or your friend group, you are not the only target to the devil; you **all** are. The most susceptible to demonic time bombs are the most dangerous people to be around, unless you have been sent to them by God, with Holy Spirit and prayerful covering.

> Praying always with all prayer and supplication in the Spirit, being watchful to this end with all perseverance and supplication for all the saints
>
> Redeeming the time because the days are evil. (Ephesians 5:16)

You are to defuse the bomb in any day, week, month, or year. There are potential dangers in each day, and it is through commanding type prayers that we can escape harm.

Command the day; tomorrow has sufficient trouble unto itself.

If you don't have the **Holy Spirit** – pray, ask for the infilling. Pray with someone who does whenever you can. Corporate prayer is a mighty weapon. Pray always. Daily. Nightly. Even if you don't need the prayer today, it's in the queue – prayers *transcend* space and time. It is better to pray a prayer that you don't need, than to not pray a prayer that you do need. Pray.

Pray, It's Your Birthday

Some bombs are timed and targeted at certain events in a person's life. A bomb may target a marriage. it can be timed for when you start to have children, or, when you graduate from school. If it's from the devil, it's whatever will bring you the most distress and destruction.

Sometimes life will go well until one day it's as though everything breaks loose. Suddenly, difficulties and complications show up in life and negative cycles begin. I've heard people say they used to enjoy the favor of God, but now they don't. This life is now put on the clock of destruction, which is obviously the devil's clock and an anti-destiny clock. That is one thing peculiar to a time bomb it has a clock or other time-keeping mechanism attached to it. The devil is not *randomly* doing things to people, he is a strategist and a planner, therefore our prayers need to be targeted, strategy-filled, timed, and timely. Powerful, prevailing prayers are needed--, immediately.

As stated, demonic bombs can be set for any day, week, month, or year. This is why we command the nights, we command the mornings, we command the day, we command the month, and we especially pray at *crossover times,* in the Name of Jesus. We **pray** every day, but it is especially critical to pray leading up to and on birthdays, anniversaries, special occasions, and so on.

People love to take time off from work and do special things on their birthday. You may have heard your mother complain of how many hours she was in labor to get you here.

Seriously, if you had any idea of the warfare involved in your parents even getting together, getting married, conceiving, carrying and giving birth to you, you'd never take a birthday for granted again. Don't curse the day you were born, but some reverence is due here.

Furthermore, a lot of religions don't even celebrate birthdays and according to Google, birthdays started out as pagan observances. Christians didn't commemorate birthdays. But do you think the greeting card and cake people would just let billions of birthdays go by—every year? Year after year??

The way to make your birthday important, meaningful, victorious is to PRAY. Birthdays, anniversaries, dates that are special to you are famous devil dates for time bomb detonation and destruction. On those occasions, people are partying and living it up. They may be a bit careless, but hopefully not prayerless. The trauma the devil would inflict is bad enough, but he hopes to get more impact on a special day. How many people remember some of their worst memories as they are associated with holidays and special dates? The devil loves to inflict trauma. Losses, especially on special dates, are usually never forgotten.

It was twelve noon on my birthday in my 20's. I was riding along in a car thinking fantastic birthday and life thoughts. I had just hung a gallery of my art in a local bookstore. My first "gallery" exhibition.

Suddenly my car got nearly t-boned by an old lady driving a hulking Chrysler. Because of physical trauma I missed months and months from work.

This was on my birthday – **sober**. The driver of my car was sober. Old lady in the big, time bomb car was also deemed sober by the police. It was my birthday.

Looking back, I'm pretty sure my destiny clock did not include the pain and loss of work. But wherever you find yourself, use that time to get closer to God.

Don't let that pain be in vain.

Destiny Clock

There is <u>one</u> **Destiny Clock** for a man and 13 counterfeit clocks. One such false clock is the clock of destruction. What do you think happens when you're thrust into the devil's timeline?

Are you *in* Christ, in the Lord's timeline? Are you where you should be, or are you out from under covering??? You could be in a successful career, making all kinds of bank, **but that doesn't necessarily mean that you are on the clock of your destiny.** You could be on a clock of *man*—, doing what you want, your own way. You could be doing what your parents, who wanted to make sure you made enough money to take care of yourself, said for you to do.

Peer pressure most often relies on the clock of man.

Time bombs are set on satanic calendar, or satanic clocks. If the devil doesn't take you out with a time bomb, he certainly tries to change the calendar and the clock you're on and put you on his timeline. In this way he tries to change the trajectory of your life, and it is not toward destiny, it is away from it. As long as you're on the devil's timeline, going by his clock, his plan, you will be where *he* wants you, when he wants you there, with whom he wants you to be with. DANGER!

In God is where your protection is. Sin pulls you down from being seated with Christ Jesus in heavenly places to being **on the same level as the enemy who wants to attack you.**

The devil is running places that are outside of God and God's timing for your life. If you remain on your clock of destiny, you'll be in right places at right times. In right places, *in Christ,* you are protected, under the shadow of His wings, in the cleft of the Rock.

Suddenly

I remember driving on that same street or a street very near where that Chrysler crashed into my car, on a one-way street with two lanes, some months earlier. That day, I felt my steering wheel pull to the right – I almost struggled with it because it didn't feel as if *I* had full control over the vehicle, but not in a scary way. I recall wondering what was that pull on my steering wheel, it was gentle but firm at the same time. It lasted a few seconds, maybe 3 to 5 seconds, but long enough for me to notice it.

It was only after the steering wheel became passive again that I noticed a vehicle to my left *in* my lane with me. Then that car swerved back into its lane and sped past me. GLORY

TO GOD. Lord, I thank You! I praise You, Lord! **Jesus took the wheel.** YES! Won't He do it. He did it for me. More than once!!! Look at that: What the devil intended for harm, God said, NO!!!

You too can probably think of instances in your life where things blew up in your face, or you were blindsided by the devil's tactics. The ownness is on me. So, I must ask myself, *What was I doing then? Was I really in Christ, or was I just halfway in, or not in at all???* Was I dwelling in the Shadow of the Almighty? What in my life, what about me *allowed* the devil to get to me???

Lord, let my soul escape as a bird from the snare. (Psalm 124:7).

Thank You, Lord: as my God lives, I will escape the enemy's time bombs. The snare of the enemy shall be ineffective against my life, in the Name of Jesus.

Every satanic time bomb planted for me in any hidden place, be revealed to me before you have a chance to detonate, in the Name of Jesus, Amen.

God reveals His secrets to the prophets. He will not do anything unless He first reveals it to the prophets. Prophets are those who speak the Word of God. Many times what God is revealing to you is for you to prophesy to yourself. Prophesy the Word, speak the Word over your own life and your own situations, so what God intends for you comes to pass instead of what the enemy desires for you.

Furthermore, some of this *revealing* happens in your dreams. If something bad appears in your dreams and you do nothing about it, that gives **approval** for that thing to come into your life.

If something good appears in your dreams, you need to pray it *through* so it can bypass obstacles that the devil will automatically set up against you, so that blessing can come to pass in your life. You have to know though is when a dream is good and when it is bad; dreams are not always literal.

Prayers

Lord. in the Name of Jesus I repent for my sins, sins of omission, commission, sins of my parents and my ancestors going back before Adam & Eve. Lord, I renounce my having sinned and every evil covenant that was formed because of my sin; I break those covenants now, in Jesus' Name. Lord, forgive me, and wash away all sin and iniquity by the Blood of Jesus. Amen.

Lord, forgive me if I have ever played a part in forming any demonic time bomb or other weapon against another living soul at any time in my life, in Jesus' Name.

Lord, let there be found nothing lacking in me that would give the enemy any reason to attack, in Jesus' Name.

All Satanic agents assigned to plant time bombs against me, be destroyed by the bomb that you are planning to use against me. Before you ever reach me, anyone or anything I have stewardship over, let it blow up in your face, in the Name of Jesus.

Angelic Bomb Squad of the Lord, seek and find every time bomb in my near or distant future and dismantle it, in the Name of Jesus! Thank You, Lord.

Teach me, by Your Spirit, Lord that I do not get tricked or ensnared again, in the Name of Jesus.

Every demonic snare set for my soul, catch your owner, in the Name of Jesus. Return to sender, 7-fold, in Jesus' Name.

Every kind of bait on the demonic trap, all bait--, food, money, get rich quick schemes, <u>free</u> stuff, honey pots-- become **<u>unattractive</u>** to my attention in the Name of Jesus. Lord, deliver me from worldly lusts, in Jesus' Name.

Spirit of the Living God, reveal the traps, snares, nets, pits and time bombs of the enemy against me, *to* me whenever and wherever they are set, in the Name of Jesus.

Every Satanic terrorist and evil human persecutor intent on devastating my life and destiny, be destroyed by Heavenly ambush, in the Name of Jesus.

Every chosen date and time to activate tragedy for my life and family, be **cancelled** before the occurrence, in the Name of Jesus. I break your assignment, I break your appointment, I break your assignment, I break your appointment, in the Name of Jesus!

Every time bomb along my path in life, Light of God that lights my path: expose them and be supernaturally defused, in the mighty Name of Jesus.

Angel of Mercy, locate any and every demonic explosive planned against me and defuse it immediately as it is planted, in the Name of Jesus.

Every Satanic agent assigned to plant bombs against my life, die on the spot, nowhere near me, in the mighty Name of Jesus, Amen.

Every power sponsoring any kind of time bomb against my life and destiny, fall down and die by Thunder, in Jesus Name.

Every demonic terrorist planning to set time bombs for my life and family, be destroyed by Thunder as you are planning your evil, in Jesus' Name.

Oh Lord my God. Ambush the Satanic terrorists on suicide missions against my life and home, in the Name of Jesus. Send seek and destroy angelic missiles through God's Warrior Angels, in Jesus' Name.

Lord, by Your Spirit reveal to me the plans of the enemy against me, in the Name of Jesus. Guard me in the places and times of danger and entrapment, in the Name of Jesus.

Show me where the Arameans have set up an ambush for me, in Jesus' Name.

Let me know by Your Spirit, or show me in Your Word, or send Word by Your Prophets, as Elisha warned the king, in times of war, in the Name of Jesus.

Lord, set the enemy on edge wondering how I know their secret plans against me, intimidate them. Make them turn against themselves, in the Name of Jesus.

Defend me, Lord from the horses, the horsemen and chariots that may arise against me, in the Name of Jesus.

Empower me, Lord, no matter what I see in the spirit, even if it be an army with horses and chariots, that I will fear not, knowing that there are more with me, than those that are against me, in the Name of Jesus.

Open my eyes, Lord, that I see how Great You Are, in Jesus' Name.

Lord, "Strike the enemy against me with blindness, in the Name of Jesus.

Mighty angels of God take captive all who are against me and lead them away; take them to where the True Lord Jesus has for them, in the Name of Jesus that they trouble me no more. Amen.

Have the bands of the enemy stop attacking me, in the Name of Jesus. (X5)

Angel of Mercy, move faster than my enemies whenever they have been sent out against me, in Jesus' Name.

Lord, You see all, You know all. You sit upon many waters. Thunder and terminate the activities of the evil bombers around my life and home, in the Name of Jesus.

Lord, build a wall of Fire, a hedge of Fire, a mountain of Fire around me, in the Name of Jesus. My life, receive Fire, become Fire, in the Name of Jesus.

Let the Fire of the Lord incinerate every time bomb against my life and destiny before it has a chance to explode, in the Name of Jesus.

Oh Lord, frustrate the activities of demonic terrorists against my household, in the Name of Jesus.

Every satanic time bomb against me or my household, be defused before the timer gets to zero, in Jesus' Name.

Every power that wants to destroy or hinder my progress in life, be destroyed by Holy Ghost Fire, in the Name of Jesus.

Every devil in stealth mode to set traps against my life and destiny, be found out. Light of God shine on them, expose them, and cast them out of my life, in the Name of Jesus.

I undo the enemy's calendar, and clock for every hour, day, week, month, and year that has been chosen for evil to strike me or my life by the power, in the Blood of Jesus.

Every evil program against me, be deprogrammed by the will of God for my life, in the Name of Jesus.

Every targeted time and event of my life for evil bombing, be rescinded by the Word of God over my life, in the Name of Jesus.

Every weapon of the enemy, be destroyed, be annihilated by the weapons from the mighty armory of God, in Jesus' Name.

Every tragedy planned for a particular date or event of my life, be averted and aborted by the power in the Blood of Jesus.

Angels of God's protection, supervise the events of my life, in Jesus' Name.

My spirit, soul, and body, be empowered to escape satanic traps and snares planted for any time of my existence, in the Name of Jesus.

Every snare and trap planned and planted for my spirit, soul and/or body, break now by Thunder, in the Name of Jesus.

Lord, my God, provide all antidotes for demonic poisons, known and unknown, in the Name of Jesus.

Lord, God of Mercy, immunize me against demonic poisons and time bombs, in the Name of Jesus.

Oh Lord, my God, let the light of Your presence both expose and scare away the demonic bomb planters, in the Name of Jesus.

Oh Lord my God, empower me to jump over the traps and snares of the enemy wherever they are planted.

> For by thee I have run through a troop;
> and by my God have I leaped over a wall.
> (Psalm 18:29)

God of Mercy, let my guardian angels to keep watch over my life against demonic time bombs, in Jesus' Name.

Holy Ghost, consume planters of time bombs, against me, in Jesus' Name.

My life is hidden in Christ and Christ is *in God*-- So I'm safe and secure from sudden calamity, in the Name of Jesus. (Colossians 3:3).

Marine spirits – python, octopus spirits whose time bomb is the wrap and the squeeze--, Father God, I request a divorce, from any *marine spirit* putting a squeeze on me or planning such on me, or any part of my life, by the Power in the Blood of Jesus. I am in Christ, and He is in me:

Release me and let me go and return to me no more, in the Name of Jesus.

Job 5:19-27 From six calamities he will rescue you; in seven no harm will touch you. In famine he will deliver you from death, and in battle from the stroke of the sword.
You will be protected from the lash of the tongue, and need not fear when destruction comes.
You will laugh at destruction and famine, and need not fear the wild animals.
For you will have a covenant with the

stones of the field,
and the wild animals will be at peace
with you.
You will know that your tent is secure;
**you will take stock of your property
and find nothing missing.**
You will know that your children will be
many, and your descendants like the grass
of the earth. Amen.

Lord, any damage or loss due to anything already exploded or imploded in my life, I ask that You restore, mend, repair the breach created by demonic time bombs, in Jesus' Name.

Lord, Your Word requires that the enemy restores to me 7-fold of all that has been stolen from me. I request it. I require it, in the Name of Jesus.

Lord, let me reach destiny, peace and prosperity, in the Name of Jesus.

I will not fear, everywhere my foot shall tread, the LORD shall give it to me. I will step forward, I will move forward in life, I will progress and reach destiny, in the Name of Jesus.

I bind and paralyze every *spirit*, power, principality who would seek retaliation against me or anyone praying these prayers, in the Name of Jesus.

Lord, thank You for answering prayer, in the Name of Jesus.

I seal these words, decrees and declarations across every realm, dimension, age, and timeline, past present and future, to infinity, in the Name of Jesus. **AMEN**.

Christian books by this author:
AK: Adventures of the Agape Kid

AMONG SOME THIEVES

As My Soul Prospers

Behave

Churchzilla (Wanna-Be Bride of Christ)

The Coco-So-So Correct Show

Demonic Cobwebs

Demonic Time Bombs

Demons Hate Questions

Do Not Orphan Your Seed

Do Not Work for Money

Don't Refuse Me Lord

Every Evil Bird

The FAT Demons

got Money?

Let Me Have a Dollar's Worth

Living for the NOW of God

Lord, Help My Debt

Lose My Location

Made Perfect In Love

The Man Safari *(I'm Just Looking)*

Marriage Ed., *Rules of Engagement & Marriage*

Motherboard: *Key to Soul Prosperity*

My Life As A Slave

Name Your Seed

Plantation Souls

The Poor Attitudes of Money

Power Money: Nine Times the Tithe

The Power of Wealth

Seasons of Grief

Seasons of War

SOULS in Captivity

Soul Prosperity: Your Health & Your Wealth

The *spirit* of Poverty

This Is *NOT* That

The Throne of Grace, *Courtroom Prayers*

Warfare Prayer Against Poverty

When the Devourer is Rebuked

The Wilderness Romance

Other Journals & Devotionals by this author:

The Cool of the Day – Journal
got HEALING? Verses for Life
got HOPE? Verses for Life
got WISDOM? Verses for Life
got GRACE? Verses for Life
got JOY? Verses for Life
got LOVE? Verses for Life
He Hears Us, Prayer Journal
I Have A Star, Dream Journal
I Have A Star, Guided Prayer Journal,
J'ai une Etoile, Journal des Reves
Let Her Dream, Dream Journal *in colors*
Men Shall Dream, Dream Journal,
My Favorite Prayers *(in 4 styles)*
My Sowing Journal
Tengo una Estrella, Diario de Sueños

Illustrated children's books by Dr. Miles
Big Dog (8-book series)
Do Not Say That to Me
Every Apple

Fluff the Clouds
I Love You All Over the World
Imma Dance
The Jump Rope
Kiss the Sun
The Masked Man
Not During a Pandemic
Push the Wind
Tangled Taffy
What If?
Wiggle, Wiggle; Giggle, Giggle
Worry About Yourself
You Did Not Say Goodbye to Me

www.ingramcontent.com/pod-product-compliance
Lightning Source LLC
Chambersburg PA
CBHW061336040426
42444CB00011B/2943